HAPPIER

Finding Your Sweet Spot In A Busy World

FRVEN LIM

WHAD-FLYT.com
FRVEN.com

HAPPIER: Finding Your Sweet Spot In A Busy World

Copyright © 2025 Frven Lim
First published in 2025

All rights reserved. No part of this book may be reproduced, stored in a retrieval system, or transmitted by any means (electronic, mechanical, photocopying, recording, or otherwise) without written permission from the author.

Because of the dynamic nature of the Internet, any web addresses or links contained in this book may have changed since publication and may no longer be valid. The information in this book is based on the author's experiences and opinions. The views expressed in this book are solely those of the author and do not necessarily reflect the views of the publisher; the publisher hereby disclaims any responsibility for them.

The author of this book does not dispense any form of medical, legal, financial, or technical advice either directly or indirectly. The intent of the author is solely to provide information of a general nature to help you in your quest for personal development and growth. In the event you use any of the information in this book, the author and the publisher assume no responsibility for your actions. If any form of expert assistance is required, the services of a competent professional should be sought.

Other books by Frven Lim:

Wellbeing + Happiness thru' Architecture + Design
*ISBN: 978-1-76124-130-7
First published 2023

Companion and Study Guide for The Happiness Advantage
First published 2024

Happier Architects: Strategies for Meaning, Success and Wellbeing
ASIN: B0DXB8J7V5
First published 2025

Further Publications (*Frven Lim as Editor-in-chief)

project 2050
2014 (*ISBN: 978-981-09-2224-5)

Crafting Public Realms
2014 (*ISBN: 978-981-09-0225-4)

1degNorth
2013 (*ISBN: 978-981-07-7534-6)

Housing People
2012 (*ISBN: 978-981-07-1793-3)

Table of Contents

Introduction

1.	The Corner Table	12
2.	Noise and Numbness	16
3.	The Question That Won't Leave	20
4.	The Invisible Drain	25
5.	Circle One: Joy	29
6.	Circle Two: Strengths	33
7.	Circle Three: Contribution	38
8.	Mapping the Overlap	43
9.	Small Shifts, Big Changes	48
10.	Melissa's Rage	52
11.	The Quiet Rhythm	58
12.	The Setback	62
13.	New Blueprints	67
14.	A Purpose Written	71
15.	Your Turn	75

Going Forward	80
Worksheets 1-4	84

Introduction

This Story is About You (Even If It Isn't)

You may not know Elena.
You may not be an architect, or a banker, or a lawyer like the characters you'll meet in these pages.

But I have a feeling you'll recognise parts of yourself in them — maybe more than you expect.

You'll recognise the long weeks.

The full calendar and the empty tank.

The constant demand to keep performing, fixing, proving, smiling.

The subtle fear that if you stop moving, the whole thing might collapse — including you.

You'll recognise the questions whispered in quiet moments:

"Is this it?"
"Why doesn't this feel like success?"
"What if I'm building a life that looks good... but doesn't fit?"

This book doesn't begin with answers.
It begins with honesty.

Why This Isn't Just a Story

Yes, what follows is a fictional narrative. But it's grounded in real conversations, real coaching frameworks, and real emotional truths I've encountered again and again — in the lives of high-achieving professionals who are secretly stretched too thin, quietly craving alignment.

It's not a step-by-step self-help manual.

But it is a guided path.

Each chapter reveals more than just a storyline — it reflects back a set of universal themes:
- Burnout that masquerades as success
- Joy forgotten in pursuit of productivity
- Natural strengths undervalued or ignored
- The quiet cost of living a life that doesn't quite fit
- And the radical idea that transformation starts not with reinvention — but with realignment

What This Story Offers You

Elena's journey mirrors what many of us go through when we start questioning the path we're on — and daring to ask: what if there's a better way?

Throughout the book, you'll see how she:
- Begins reconnecting with what brings her alive
- Names her strengths — the ones that often go unseen
- Reclaims her right to meaningful work and financial sustainability
- And gently reweaves a life that finally feels like hers

This story will give you language.
It will offer permission.

And if you choose to engage with the reflective prompts and companion tools, it will also offer you a roadmap back to your own sweet spot — the place where joy, skill, purpose, and sustainability overlap.

———

One Last Thing Before We Begin

You don't need to be "burned out enough" to deserve change.

You don't need to have it all figured out before you take the first step.

You don't need to become someone new.

You just need to be willing to return — to the part of you that always knew:

You were meant for more than performance.
You were meant for alignment.
You were meant to feel alive in your own life.

If that's where you are — then this story is for you.

Let's begin.

— Frven

Something's Missing...

Chapter 1
The Corner Table

She was ten minutes early, which almost never happened anymore.

Elena sat down at the corner table out of habit — second from the window, left side, slightly hidden. It was the same one she used to sit at in grad school when she was working on her thesis models. Back when she carried an actual sketchbook and not four devices and an executive title.

The café had changed. She had changed. But somehow, this little corner felt like the only thing that hadn't been redrawn a dozen times.

She opened her planner. Not the sleek digital one. The real one. Paper. The kind she swore she'd stop using but never did.

Meeting at 4:30. Budget review. Client follow-up. Prep for Monday's town hall. Team one-on-one. Parent-teacher conference. Backlog. Feedback loop.
Her eyes blurred.

The latte was already cooling, untouched. She picked it up, then put it back down. No appetite. No real desire to drink anything. Her jaw ached, clenched like it had been all week. She realised she was grinding her teeth again. That had come back.

She took a breath. Then another.

Her phone buzzed — Slack. Email. Another ping. She turned it over.

Something inside her was tired. Not end-of-the-day tired. Worn-out tired.
The kind of tired that didn't go away with sleep. The kind that came from living off adrenaline and responsibility for too long.
And now, that strange and dangerous quiet had started to show up.
Not just exhaustion — emptiness.

She used to feel lit up by her work. Urban design was never just a job. It was shaping spaces, creating feeling, shaping cities that shaped people. At least it used to be.

Now, it felt like all she was shaping were decks. PowerPoint. Politics.
She was managing everything — except her own life.

Her shoulders sank into the café seat as if her body wanted to disappear into the foam. She blinked hard. She wasn't going to cry. Not here.

A barista walked past with a broom, smiling politely. Elena nodded. She wondered if they knew how many people sat in this spot quietly falling apart.

Her hand instinctively opened the planner again. Not to look at anything. Just muscle memory.

And that's when she noticed it — something she'd scribbled in the corner of yesterday's page, in her own handwriting:

"What if this isn't burnout? What if it's misalignment?"

She stared at it.

She didn't remember writing it.

But it felt like someone had left a note for her —
someone who knew.

Chapter 2
Noise and Numbness

She didn't remember walking to the office, only arriving there.

The lift ride to the 21st floor felt like a tunnel — the kind where you're moving but not arriving, nodding but not quite awake. When the doors opened, the usual overstimulated hum of open-plan urgency greeted her: heels clicking on vinyl, the predictable sighs of someone asking for "just five more minutes," the pings of Slack messages chasing after every second of stillness.

She walked to her desk, dropped her laptop bag gently onto the side table like a ritual offering, and sat down.

"Morning, boss," came a voice from over the divider.

It was Jamie — efficient, ever-cheerful, barely thirty, and somehow surviving off oat milk and boundless optimism.

Elena managed a smile. "Morning."

Jamie continued talking — something about the project timeline, how the stakeholder had changed their mind again, and whether she still wanted the team to present next week or delay. Elena nodded and made agreeable sounds, all the while hearing none of it.

Her mind kept circling back to the words she'd written the day before:

What if this isn't burnout? What if it's misalignment?

She didn't remember writing it, but now it sat in her chest like a question she couldn't un-ask.

She opened her calendar — not to check anything, just to look at it. It was packed. She could see exactly where her energy would go for the next six days. Nowhere in it was a pause. No white space. No room to breathe.

There was a time she would have felt pride in that.

There was a time when she wanted to fill every square centimetre of her time — to matter, to move, to prove.

Now, it just looked like a spreadsheet of slow collapse.

Her phone buzzed again.

This time, it was a voice note.

Melissa. Her sister. The lawyer.

She swiped it open.

"Okay, you're going to laugh, but I just spent twenty minutes crying in the bathroom at work because I can't remember why I'm doing any of this. Like, I know what I do. I know I'm good at it. I know how much I make. But I don't know why I'm still doing this day after day when every cell in my body just wants to stop."

A pause.

"Is this normal? Is this what being a grown-up is? Because I swear, if one more person tells me to take a bubble bath and journal, I'm going to scream."

Elena pressed pause.

She stared at the grey-blue skyline outside her window.

She wasn't the only one.
That somehow made her feel better. And worse.

Chapter 3
The Question That Won't Leave

"You want wine?" Melissa asked, already pouring.

Elena nodded, half-laughing. "Is that even a question tonight?"

They were at Luca's, the kind of modern Italian place where the lights were just dim enough to look forgiving and the tables just close enough to feel like someone was always eavesdropping.

They used to come here for birthdays. Celebrations. Wins.

Tonight, it felt like they were here for something else — something harder to name.

Melissa sat across from her in a tailored blazer, makeup sharp, posture military. Elena wondered how many people in her firm thought she had it all together. How many saw the emails at 2:14 a.m. and thought, "She's a machine."

She had no idea her sister cried in the office bathroom.

"So," Melissa began, swirling her glass, "I sent you that voice note. Sorry for the emotional ambush."

"No," Elena said quickly. "It was... honest."

Melissa exhaled. "I've been spinning for months. Like... I'm good at this. You know? I can write briefs in my sleep. I close deals, I win cases, I get praise. But it's like the more I achieve, the less it means."

Elena nodded, too fast. "Yes. Exactly."

"Then I look around and think, okay — maybe I'm the problem. Maybe I'm just ungrateful. Maybe it's burnout and I need to take a holiday and drink a smoothie."

They both laughed. It was the first sound of lightness all evening.

Elena reached into her tote bag and pulled out her planner.

She flipped it open to the page she couldn't stop thinking about.

"What if this isn't burnout? What if it's misalignment?"

Melissa read it. Twice.

Then looked up, slower this time. "Damn."

"Right?"

"I mean…" She leaned back. "Yeah. That actually lands."

They both sat in silence for a moment, the noise of the restaurant buzzing around them like static.

"You think we're in the wrong life?" Melissa asked quietly.

Elena didn't answer right away. She looked down at her wine. Then her hands.

"I think," she said slowly, "we stopped asking the right questions a long time ago. Or maybe we never learned to ask them in the first place."

Melissa leaned in, eyes softening. "So what do we do?"

Elena smiled, just a little. "I don't know. But I think we start here. With this."

She pointed at the scribble in her planner. Misalignment.

It wasn't a diagnosis. It wasn't a solution.

But it was a start.

Chapter 4
The Invisible Drain

Elena sat on her balcony that Saturday morning with no meetings, no calls, and — for the first time in weeks — no urgent emails screaming at her from a glowing screen.

Just a cup of strong black coffee. A blank page. And a pen.

The city stretched beyond her railing, quiet in its weekend hush. The only sound was the slow whir of the ceiling fan, which made her plants dance lazily in the morning sun.

She opened her planner and flipped past project lists and strategy diagrams until she landed on a fresh spread.

At the top of the page, in her own handwriting, she'd written:

Daily Joy Inventory.
What brought me energy this week?

It felt like a strange question to ask herself — like a luxury. Maybe even self-indulgent.

But then she remembered what Melissa had said over dinner.

"Maybe we never learned to ask the right questions."

She exhaled. Picked up her pen.

She began to write, hesitantly at first:
- Tuesday morning, walking to the bakery alone. No headphones. Just birds and sunlight.
- Laughing with Jamie during that ridiculous Zoom bug.
- Sketching out the community proposal by hand, just for fun.
- Helping Layla prep her internship presentation. Seeing her beam.

She stopped. Looked at the list.

It surprised her.

None of those things were part of her "real job." None of them were billable. None had KPIs or productivity tied to them.

And yet... they were the moments where she felt present. Light. Alive.

She turned the page.

Energy Audit.
What drained me this week?

This list came faster.
- Budget review with Finance.
- Back-to-back Zooms with no air.
- Explaining — for the fourth time — the same feedback to the same person.
- Reading industry updates at midnight like it was oxygen.
- Smiling through another "just one more request" from the client who never respected boundaries.

She paused again. This list felt heavier. More familiar.

She stared at both pages side by side — joy vs. drain.
It was like reading two versions of her life.

And the question returned, sharper now:

What if this isn't burnout? What if it's misalignment?

For the first time, it didn't just sound poetic.

It sounded obvious.

Chapter 5
Circle One: Joy

It was Wednesday when Elena decided to walk to work.

Not for the steps. Not for the environment. Not even because her car was blocked in again.

She walked because something inside her wanted to move — not efficiently, not productively — but intentionally.
Like a person, not a professional.

No headphones. No emails. Just city rhythm and morning light.

The sky was sharp blue, and even the traffic seemed to part for her. As she passed the corner florist, the smell of jasmine hit her so suddenly she stopped in her tracks. She stood there for a moment, smiling like someone who remembered an inside joke from years ago.

And just like that — joy.

Not performative, not strategic. Just real.

———

At lunch, she said no to three meeting requests and took her food outside to a bench overlooking the river.

She opened her planner, flipped to her Joy Inventory page, and added:
- Jasmine outside the flower shop.
- Walking without multitasking.
- Saying no without guilt.

It felt small. But real.

Later that night, Melissa sent her a text:

"I tried your little joy inventory thing. Turns out coffee in silence is better than I thought. Also, I deleted LinkedIn for a week. That counts, right?"

Elena laughed aloud. Typed back:

"Counts triple. Bonus points if you light a candle and pretend you live in a cabin."

Then, another message came through — from Andre.

She hadn't heard from him in months.

"Hey, random question. Do you ever feel like you built exactly the life you wanted — and now can't remember why you wanted it?"

She stared at it for a long time.

There it was again.

That strange little echo from all directions — as if people were quietly waking up from the same dream.

———

That night, Elena made herself a simple dinner. No screens. No emails.

She lit a candle — just one — and played a piano playlist she hadn't touched in years.

She didn't call it self-care. She didn't call it healing.

She just called it Wednesday.

Chapter

Circle Two: Strengths

Elena never thought a junior presentation could leave her holding back tears.

It wasn't the content — it was Layla.

She watched her young intern walk through her first community design proposal, hands shaking slightly, voice a little too fast, but heart completely in it.

And when she reached the last slide — a beautifully hand-drawn visualisation of a public square filled with plants, laughter, shade and strangers resting shoulder to shoulder — Layla looked up and smiled, as if the future was something she could already see.

The room clapped. Lightly. Politely.

But Elena didn't just clap. She paused.

Because for that moment, she could see it too.

After the meeting, Layla came over.

"Thanks for pushing me," she said. "You're a really good mentor. You make things feel… safe. But sharp."

Elena smiled. "Safe but sharp?"

Layla grinned. "Like, you'll challenge my thinking, but not shame me for not knowing."

It was such an offhand compliment — a throwaway kindness — but it landed with weight.

Because Elena couldn't remember the last time she thought of that as a strength.

In her world, sharpness was often mistaken for cold. And safety… was rarely celebrated at all.

She flipped open her planner that night.

Circle Two: Strengths
What comes naturally to me, even when I'm not trying?

She started writing:
- Seeing the big picture.
- Translating chaos into clarity.
- Holding space without softening the truth.
- Noticing what people don't say.
- Drawing out potential in others.

It felt strange to put those down. Like admitting something that might be used against her.

But it also felt like… telling the truth.

The next day, she met Andre for coffee.

He looked good, in that polished-but-fraying-around-the-edges way most successful men in finance eventually did. Clean suit, tired eyes. Laughing too loudly at nothing. Checking his phone between every sentence.

"You're glowing," he said, mock-serious. "Did you go off-grid and discover meditation?"

She smiled. "Something like that."

They talked about work, old friends, new promotions, the usual updates. Until eventually, the performance wore off and Andre sighed.

"You ever wonder if you're just… climbing a really tall ladder," he said, "only to realise it's leaning against the wrong wall?"

Elena blinked. "That's exactly it."

He nodded slowly. "I've spent fifteen years getting better and better at something I'm not sure I even like. I'm respected. I'm promoted. I'm... miserable."

Elena tilted her head. "What are you actually good at? Like, naturally?"

He smiled, caught off guard. "You're pulling out the coaching voice now."

She didn't reply. Just raised her eyebrows.

Andre looked away for a moment.

"I think I'm good at getting people to move," he said. "Not just in terms of deals. I mean... helping them make decisions. Helping them cut through the noise."

She nodded. "That's a strength."

He looked down. "Doesn't feel like one anymore."

Chapter 7
Circle Three: Contribution

Elena had barely stepped out of the elevator when she heard the sound:
Raised voices. Tension. The unmistakable thump of a rolled-up drawing hitting a table too hard.

She followed the noise into one of the break-out rooms.

Two junior team members — Amir and Zoe — were in the middle of what looked like a poorly disguised meltdown over a public housing presentation. Words were spilling faster than either of them could catch. Something about deadlines. Revisions. A lack of "real input from the community."

When they noticed her, they fell silent.

"Sorry," Amir said. "We're just—"
"—trying to do it properly," Zoe added, jaw clenched. "But it feels like it doesn't matter."

Elena looked at the sketch on the table. It was technically fine. Efficient. Neat. Completely devoid of life.

"Tell me," she said calmly, "what you wanted this to do."

They hesitated. Then Zoe pulled out a small notebook and flipped to a scribbled page: a series of hand-drawn notes from interviews with residents — mostly elderly — about their hopes for the redesigned plaza.

"Shade. Safety. More benches. A place for the kids to run. Somewhere to sit that doesn't feel like you're loitering."

Zoe paused. "It's not in the proposal. None of it."

Elena looked at her. And then Amir.

"Do you think our job is to design something that looks good on a PDF?" she asked.

They didn't answer.

"Or is it to shape space so it feels like home?"

Still nothing. Just a slow, quiet shame washing across their faces.

She softened. "Do the version that matters. You've got three days. I'll cover the delay."

Their eyes widened.

"Really?"

"Really."

That night, Elena sat with her planner again.

Circle Three: Contribution
Where does my work actually make a difference — and to whom?

She wrote:
- When I let younger voices be heard
- When I remind others why we build
- When I protect space for people, not just projects
- When I help something feel more human

She stared at the last one.

That's what had been missing all along.

She hadn't felt human in her work for months — and so nothing she made could feel that way either.

Two days later, the team presented a new version of the housing proposal.
It wasn't flashy. But it was beautiful in a quiet way — shaded seating, thoughtful paths, a playground tucked near the community garden. A design not for awards, but for use.

Afterwards, one of the senior partners leaned over to Elena.

"Not the most exciting scheme," he muttered, "but I guess it'll get approval."

Elena just smiled.

Because the older man who shuffled into the town hall later that week, stared at the render, and whispered "That looks like my street"?
He didn't care about excitement.
He saw himself in it.

And that was the kind of impact no brief could measure.

Chapter

Mapping the Overlap

The café was half-empty, which is exactly how Elena liked it.

She ordered her usual — oat latte, extra shot — and took the corner table by the window. Not her old spot. A new one. She liked the symbolism.

She opened her planner and flipped back to the past three weeks.

Joy. Strengths. Contribution.

It looked like a quiet revolution on paper.
Moments scribbled in blue ink. Small epiphanies in the margins.
The kinds of things you don't think matter until you realise they're your life.

She turned to a blank page and drew three circles.

In the first, she wrote:

Joy
- Sketching without pressure
- Walking slowly
- Mentoring
- Silence before the city wakes up

In the second:

Strengths
- Translating chaos into clarity
- Reading between the lines
- Creating space for others to grow

In the third:

Contribution
- Humanising public spaces
- Protecting younger voices
- Helping people feel seen

She stared at the centre. The implied sweet spot.

It was beautiful.

It was also… incomplete.

Because somewhere between the latte and the revelation, her phone had buzzed with a notification:

💸 Your credit card bill is now due. Total amount: $3,877.24.

Her breath hitched.

Rent. Groceries. Her mum's birthday trip. That dental thing she still hadn't booked.
And Layla had asked her just yesterday whether she'd consider teaching part-time at the design school.

It had made her heart flutter — in the best way. But the pay?

She flipped to the back of the notebook and scribbled:

Can I live on this?

Then circled it. Hard.

———

That evening, she called Melissa.

"I did the exercise," Elena said. "I drew the circles. It was beautiful. Until I remembered bills exist."

Melissa laughed. "Welcome to the grown-up dreamers' club."

"I feel like I finally see what I want," Elena said. "And now I have to admit — not all of it pays."

Melissa paused. "Okay. So maybe there's a fourth circle."

Elena blinked. "Go on."

"One that no one puts in the TED Talk diagrams. One that just says: What people will actually pay you to do."

Elena nodded slowly. "The financial viability circle."

"Exactly."

"And without it…"

"It's just a very poetic form of unemployment."

They both laughed, but Elena was already sketching a new diagram — this time with four circles, gently overlapping.

Joy
Strengths
Contribution
Income

The centre got smaller. But it got real.

She labelled it:

The Sustainable Sweet Spot

Chapter 9
Small Shifts, Big Changes

Elena stood outside her director's office, palms a little damp, the kind of nerves that didn't come from fear — but from doing something unfamiliar, on purpose.

She knocked.

"Come in," her boss called out.

Darren was polite. Efficient. The kind of person who appreciated results more than small talk.

"Everything okay?" he asked as she stepped in.

"Yes," Elena said, sitting down. "Actually… I'd like to talk about something before it isn't."

That got his attention.

She took a breath.

"I've been reflecting on my role. Not because I'm unhappy with the team or the projects — I care about both. But I've noticed that what energises me the most — mentoring, vision work, community engagement — has slowly taken a back seat to process, reports, and politics."

He nodded slowly. Neutral.

"I'm not asking for a restructure," she continued. "But I'd like to propose a slight shift in my responsibilities — maybe an internal mentoring programme, or taking lead on our talent development strategy. Something that lets me stay aligned with what I do best and still deliver value to the firm."

She placed a small one-page summary on his desk.

It wasn't radical. But it was intentional.

He scanned it, then looked up. "This is… thoughtful. And refreshingly clear."

She smiled. "I've been working on clarity."

———

That evening, Elena sat on her balcony again, tea in hand instead of wine this time.

She didn't know if her proposal would be accepted. But that wasn't the point.

She had taken one small step toward the centre of her circles.

And it felt good.

Later that night, her phone buzzed.

Andre.

"I had a performance review today. Hit every target. They're giving me a bonus. And I walked out of the room wondering how long I can keep doing work I've outgrown."

"Also, I started sketching again. Just for myself. First time in ten years."

Elena replied:

"Sometimes the smallest return is the biggest shift."

"More of that, Andre. That's where we start."

Chapter 10
Melissa's Rage

Melissa had never cried at work before.

Not in the early years of the firm when the pressure was brutal, not when she'd pulled her first all-nighter drafting a client memo with one eye twitching from espresso, not even when she lost a case that she knew should've gone the other way.

But today?

Today, she found herself in the unisex toilet, staring at her own reflection like it belonged to someone else.

And the tears came. Quiet. Uninvited. But also... unstoppable.

She didn't know if it was the partner who'd just given credit to someone else for her strategy, or the fact that she hadn't had a real day off in fourteen weeks, or that she had forgotten her own birthday until her mother reminded her that morning.

Maybe it was all of it.

Or maybe it was something else entirely — something deeper.

———

That night, she called Elena.

"I think I'm officially unravelled," she said into the phone.

"Are you home?" Elena asked.

"No. Still at the office. Trying to write an email I don't care about for a case I wish I wasn't on."

"Then stop. Come over."

Melissa hesitated. "You sure?"

"I'm already heating soup."

Half an hour later, they sat on Elena's couch, mismatched socks tucked under a blanket, soup bowls resting on their laps like warm shields.

"I'm so tired," Melissa said. "But more than that, I'm angry. I've built this career. This reputation. I'm good at it. I've earned the bonuses, the praise. And yet—"

She paused.

"Yet I can't remember the last time I felt proud of who I am — not what I do, not what I've won — but who I actually am."

Elena listened. No fixes. Just space.

Melissa wiped her nose, suddenly self-conscious.

"You know what's the worst part?" she whispered. "I didn't want to tell anyone. Not even you. Because I thought it would make me look weak. Like I couldn't handle it."

Elena nodded gently. "That's not weakness. That's pride."

Melissa blinked. "Excuse me?"

"El, you said it yourself. You're not crying because you're failing — you're crying because you're alone in it."

Melissa exhaled. Hard.

"We're not meant to hold all of this alone," Elena said. "We were never taught how to ask for help — only how to exceed expectations."

There was a silence. Not awkward. Just true.

Then Elena picked up a pen from the coffee table and wrote something on a sticky note:

TEAM =
Together Everyone Achieves More

Melissa rolled her eyes but smiled anyway. "Did you get that from a corporate training video?"

"Probably," Elena smirked. "But that doesn't make it less true."

She handed Melissa the note.

"Maybe part of real strength," she said, "is choosing to be seen. Letting someone sit beside you when everything feels too much."

Melissa looked at the note again. Slid it into her handbag without comment.

And somehow, that gesture — small and quiet — felt more honest than any closing argument she'd ever given in court.

Chapter 11
The Quiet Rhythm

The invitation was simple.

A group message from Elena.

"Nothing fancy. Just dinner. At mine. Saturday. 7pm. Bring something real — food, story, whatever. No networking, no agenda. Just us."

Melissa had replied within thirty seconds:

"Do emotional breakdowns count as appetisers?"

Andre took longer. His reply came an hour later.

"I'll bring wine and a question I still don't know how to answer."

Perfect.

―――

Saturday night, Elena lit candles. Not for ambience — for softness.

The table wasn't curated, just layered: pasta, bread, cut vegetables, imperfect wine glasses that clinked with comfort.

When Melissa arrived, she dropped a tote bag filled with lemon cake and sarcasm.
When Andre showed up, he brought two bottles of red and the visible relief of being somewhere that didn't require small talk.

They ate slowly.

Talked easily.

Laughed the way people do when no one's trying to prove they're okay.

―――

Later, with plates cleared and everyone curled into corners of the living room, Andre leaned forward.

"You ever notice how different the day feels when you don't start it in panic?"

Elena smiled. "I do now."

He nodded. "I've been experimenting. Mornings without screens. Stretching. Writing five sentences about what I want from the day before I get pulled into a hundred other people's versions."

Melissa sipped her wine. "I booked a three-day weekend next month. First one in two years. I already told my assistant I'm going off-grid. Even deleted Slack from my phone."

"That's basically a spiritual cleanse," Andre said.

They laughed.

Then Melissa looked at Elena.

"What about you? What's shifted?"

Elena paused. "Honestly? Less doing. More noticing. I started giving myself one hour a day where I don't owe anyone anything. No calls, no replies, no goals. Just space."

They all sat with that for a moment. How revolutionary "nothing" could feel.

Elena got up and returned with a small notepad.

"I've been drawing something. It's not finished. Just... an idea."

She opened to a sketch — four overlapping circles. At the centre: a shaded shape. Underneath, she had written:

A life that works. Because it fits.

Joy.
Strengths.
Contribution.
Sustainability.

Andre pointed to the centre. "Is that the goal?"

Elena shrugged. "Maybe not a goal. More like a compass."

Melissa smiled. "It's funny. None of us has made a huge change. And yet... everything feels different."

"Not everything," Elena said, "just the rhythm."

Chapter 12
The Setback

It started with a phone call at 6:42am.

"Elena. It's Mum. I think I need to go to the hospital."

No explanation. Just breathlessness. Panic.

Within fifteen minutes, Elena was in a cab, eyes blurry from sleep, mind racing faster than the passing streets.

The next 48 hours were a blur of waiting rooms, forms, tests, explanations no one understood the first time.

Her mother was okay — a minor cardiac event, the doctors said. Nothing irreversible. But it shook her.

It shook Elena, too.

———

By the end of the week, the quiet rhythm she'd begun to build had vanished.

She'd cancelled her one-on-ones. Missed her personal "hour of space" five days in a row.
Her Joy page hadn't been opened since Monday.
The circles in her sketchbook blurred into the bottom of her tote bag, smudged by a leaking pen and takeout receipts.

And when she finally got home one night — keys in hand, too tired to cry — she found herself standing in the middle of her living room wondering whether anything had changed at all.

———

The next morning, she sat at her kitchen table with coffee and silence.

She stared out the window. Not for clarity. Just because she couldn't stare inward anymore.

Her planner lay open, accidentally flipped to an old page. One of the first.

"What if this isn't burnout? What if it's misalignment?"

She smiled. Not because it was funny. But because it was familiar.

And in that moment, she realised something:
The difference wasn't that her life was now perfect or balanced or protected from chaos.

The difference was that she could see it now.

Before, she would have pushed through. Reached for more caffeine. Buried the discomfort in productivity.

Now? She just paused.

———

She sent a message to Andre.

"I've completely fallen out of rhythm this week. But I know how to return now. That's new."

He replied immediately:

"Falling out of rhythm is human. Remembering how to come back is growth."

———

Elena sat a little straighter.

She made a new page in her planner.

At the top, she wrote:

Return Ritual

Underneath:

- One deep breath before opening email
- 15 minutes outside with no purpose
- Write one thing I want, not just what I owe
- Text someone who reminds me who I am

Chapter 13
New Blueprints

Elena sat on the train, eyes closed, feeling the hum of forward motion.
Not rushing. Not multitasking. Just moving.

She had started taking the train again once a week. Not for efficiency, but for presence.

In her lap, she held a folder filled with lesson plans. Tonight was her third evening teaching at the design school — just one night a week, but enough to feel something had realigned.

She wasn't trying to overhaul her life anymore.

She was adjusting it — brick by brick. Breath by breath.

———

Melissa, meanwhile, had taken to walking her own court papers across the office — on purpose — just for five minutes of movement and reset between meetings.

She now kept a sticky note on her monitor:

"Perfect is not the goal. Progress is."

She had been told her whole life that practise makes perfect — and she had believed it. It had made her efficient. Impressive. Respected.

But also — brittle.

Because what no one said out loud was that "perfect" is a moving target.

It shifts. It bends. And when it stays out of reach, it makes you feel like you're always falling short — even when you're flying.

So she rewrote the phrase:

"Practise makes progress."

And that, she realised, was the real discipline:
Not flawless performance. But honest momentum.

Andre had started attending a life drawing class.

He hadn't held charcoal since college.

He wasn't great at it anymore — his hands were stiff, his proportions off. But for two hours every Thursday, he didn't think about margins, clients, or deadlines.

He just sketched.

And that was enough.

"I don't need it to be good," he told Elena once. "I just need it to be."

At dinner that week, the three of them sat at Elena's table again — mismatched plates, better wine, fewer masks.

"I realised something," Melissa said. "We spent years trying to optimise ourselves. Like we were spreadsheets."

Andre nodded. "We were taught to measure everything — except how we felt."

Elena raised her glass. "So maybe this season isn't about maximising. It's about rebalancing."

They clinked glasses.

The table was quieter than before — not because there was less to say, but because there was less to prove.

They were still learning.

Still trying.

Still getting it wrong, some days.

But more than anything, they were moving — gently, forward, together.

Chapter 14
A Purpose, Written

It was quiet at the co-working space — a typical morning hush, the kind that makes even the clatter of a coffee mug sound intentional.

Elena sat by the window, a warm breeze brushing her neck. Her notebook lay open in front of her, a clean page waiting like soft invitation.

She'd been avoiding this one — not because she didn't want to do it, but because it felt like it needed to be right.

That old instinct again: get it perfect. Nail it on the first try.

But she caught herself.

No. Progress, not perfection. That's what they had all agreed.

So she picked up her pen, exhaled slowly, and began.

At the top, she wrote:

My Purpose Statement (Version 1.0)

Then paused.

She thought about the four circles. The sketches. The conversations.
The quiet shifts. The loud rethinks.
The setbacks. The returns.

And then, slowly:

I feel most fulfilled when I use my gift for clarity and care to help others rediscover what matters — in their space, their work, or their story — and to make room for more of it.

She read it once. Then again.

It wasn't final. But it was true.

And that was enough.

―――

That evening, she sent a group message.

"Small idea. Want to each write our own first version of a purpose statement? No pressure. No polish. Just truth."

Melissa replied with a photo of a handwritten napkin. It said:

"I feel aligned when I stand for people who can't yet stand for themselves — in rooms where power forgets who it's meant to protect."

Andre followed an hour later:

"I want to help people choose better. Not just investments. But lives."

Elena smiled. These weren't taglines.

They were starting points.

―――

Later that night, she opened her laptop.

She clicked "New Document." At the top, she typed a title:

The Sweet Spot: Notes from a Realignment

And underneath:

This isn't a book about reinvention. It's about return.
To joy. To clarity. To what we forgot we were allowed to want.
To a life that fits.
One circle at a time.

She stared at it.

Then hit save.

Chapter 15
Your Turn

It started with one post.

Just a photo — her notebook open to the four circles. A small caption underneath.

Not a big revelation. Just a real one.
Sometimes the life we want isn't about changing everything.
Just remembering what matters, one circle at a time.

#thesweetspot #realignment #notperfectbutreal

Elena didn't expect anyone to notice.

But they did.

The comments came in slowly at first, then faster.

"This hit hard."
"I've been feeling this for months but didn't have the language for it."
"Do you coach? Can I learn how to do this too?"

She stared at that last one.

And something shifted.

———

That night, over tea, she read the comments out loud to Melissa and Andre.

"Maybe this wasn't just for me," she said.

Andre smiled. "Alignment has gravity."

Melissa nodded. "When we live closer to ourselves, it pulls others in. Like permission."

Elena thought about that for a long time.

Maybe the sweet spot wasn't just a private discovery.

Maybe it was a map.

And maybe, just maybe, she could help others find their way back too.

———

A Word to You, The Reader

If you're here — at the end of this story — chances are something stirred in you.

Maybe a sentence.
Maybe a character.
Maybe a quiet "yes" you didn't expect.

This story was never meant to give you all the answers.
It was meant to create a mirror. A doorway. A breath.

But now, the page turns — and it's your life that's next.

So ask yourself:
- What brings you alive?
- What do you do with ease that the world needs?
- What would it look like to make even 10% more space for that?
- And what support would help you not just imagine it… but live it?

You can walk this path on your own.

But you don't have to.

———

Why Coaching Can Help

The truth is — even the most brilliant, capable people struggle to see themselves clearly. We get tangled in old stories. Overcommitted. Under-supported. Quietly out of sync with what we once loved.

That's where coaching comes in.

A good coach won't give you answers.
But they'll ask the kind of questions that bring you back to your answers.
They'll hold space for the truth behind the noise.
They'll help you name — and claim — the life you're here to live.

And most importantly?

They'll walk beside you. Especially in the moments you're most likely to walk away from yourself.

———

Consider This Your Invitation

If this story has opened something in you — and you're ready to explore what your sweet spot looks like — I'd be honoured to guide you.

Coaching with me isn't about fixing you.

It's about helping you remember what was never broken — just buried.

Let's design something better.
Not perfect.
Just real.
And fully yours.

— Frven

Going Forward:
Why Worksheets Work (When You Commit to Them)

If you've ever worked with a great coach, you'll know how powerful it can be to have someone guide you, ask the right questions, and hold you accountable.

But what if you're not working with a coach right now?

What if you're in a moment where you want to reflect, realign, and move forward — on your own?

That's where worksheets like the ones in this book come in.

They aren't just pages to fill in — they're structured, intentional spaces for you to pause, think deeply, and reconnect with your own direction.

Why Use Worksheets?

Worksheets help you:
- Turn vague thoughts into clear insights
- Organise your reflections
- Recognise patterns you may have missed
- See how your strengths, values, and energy intersect
- Design your next steps with more intention

They offer a quiet kind of coaching — except the coach is you.

But Here's the Honest Truth

Working through these pages won't feel like a breakthrough every time.
You might hit a question that's difficult or uncomfortable.
You might be tempted to skip ahead.

And unlike a coach, a worksheet won't nudge you when you procrastinate.
It won't send you a message asking, "Did you do the thing you said you would?"

This is where self-discipline and honesty come in.

———

The Tradeoff: Flexibility vs. Accountability

With a coach, you gain external accountability — and research shows that this significantly improves your chances of follow-through. Someone else is walking beside you, keeping you on track.

With self-coaching, you gain flexibility. You move at your own pace, on your own terms. You choose the time, the setting, the mood. For many, this freedom makes reflection feel safer, even more powerful.

Both paths are valid.
Neither is better — they're just different.

———

The Good News?

When you show up honestly and consistently, these worksheets can change your life.

They can help you:
- Get clear on what matters most
- Navigate moments of change or uncertainty
- Reclaim joy and energy in your work and life
- Create a personal rhythm that feels like you
- Align your days with a deeper sense of purpose

But only if you do the work.
Not perfectly. Just consistently, courageously, and with curiosity.

―――

How to Begin

- Pick one worksheet that speaks to where you are right now.
- Set aside 20–30 minutes. (Even 10 can be enough to start.)
- Don't aim for perfection — aim for honesty.
- Revisit your answers over time. This is a process, not a one-time fix.

And if you ever want support along the way — from a real, human coach — that option will always be there. But for now, this is your space. Your pace. Your path.

Let's begin.

Worksheet 1: Discovering Your Circle of Joy

Purpose:

To help you identify the activities, moments, and experiences that bring you genuine joy.

Instructions:

- Reflect on the following questions and record your answers in detail.
- Consider the small moments in your life that make you feel most alive, and the activities that bring you joy—without external pressure or expectations.

What are the activities that make you feel completely alive, relaxed, and in the flow?
(List 3–5 activities)

Think about the last time you felt pure joy. What were you doing? Who were you with? Where were you?
(Write a brief description of the situation)

When you look back at your week, what are the moments that brought you energy and happiness?
(List 3–5 moments and why they made you happy)

What do you feel most connected to in those joyful moments (people, places, passions)?
(Reflect on the connections that amplify your joy)

How can you make more room for these joyful activities in your life going forward?
(Write down actionable steps)

Worksheet 2: Identifying Your Circle of Strengths

Purpose: To help you recognize your natural strengths and skills that empower you.

Instructions:

- Reflect on your talents, qualities, and skills. These are the aspects of yourself that come naturally and allow you to succeed.

What do others often compliment you on or ask for your help with?
(List 3–5 strengths that others frequently notice about you)

What activities do you excel at, even without much effort or practice?
(Think about areas where you feel at ease or in flow)

What strengths have helped you overcome challenges in your life or career?
(Write down examples of times your strengths carried you through difficult situations)

What do you enjoy doing that makes you feel confident and capable?
(List activities or tasks where you feel empowered and proud)

How can you intentionally use these strengths in your daily life or career to create more success and satisfaction?
(Write down 2–3 ways to leverage your strengths)

Worksheet 3: Clarifying Your Circle of Contribution

Purpose: To help you reflect on how your work and actions can contribute meaningfully to others and the world.

Instructions:

- Reflect on the impact you wish to have on others, your community, and the world.

What type of impact do you want to have in the world through your work or actions?
(Be specific about the positive change you wish to create)

What makes you feel fulfilled when you contribute to others?
(Think about the actions or situations that make you feel like you've made a difference)

Who benefits from your contributions, and how does it affect them?
(List people, communities, or causes that are impacted by your contributions)

When have you felt truly proud of something you've contributed?
(Describe a moment or project where you felt your contribution made a meaningful difference)

How can you increase your contributions in a way that aligns with your values and brings you joy?
(Write down ways you can contribute more meaningfully in the future)

Worksheet 4: Assessing Your Circle of Income

Purpose: To help you align your financial goals with your passions and values, while ensuring sustainability.

Instructions:

- Reflect on your financial goals, the value you offer through your work, and how to maintain financial sustainability while staying aligned with your values.

What financial goals do you have for your future, and how do they align with your values?
(List 2–3 short-term and long-term financial goals)

How does your current work or business generate income, and is it aligned with your purpose and passions?
(Reflect on whether your income is tied to something meaningful to you)

In what ways can you increase your income while maintaining balance and staying true to your values?
(Think of practical strategies to increase your income sustainably)

What barriers or fears are standing in the way of your financial growth, and how can you address them?
(Identify limiting beliefs or obstacles you face regarding money)

What financial steps can you take this month to move closer to a life of financial stability and fulfillment?
(Write down 2–3 actionable steps you can take right now)

Conclusion for All Worksheets:

After completing these worksheets, take time to reflect on your answers and identify the intersections between joy, strengths, contribution, and income.

Your personal **"sweet spot"** exists where these elements align. By focusing on these areas, you can create a life that is not only happier but also deeply fulfilling, purposeful, and sustainable.

These worksheets provide a structured yet introspective way for you to engage deeply with the core themes discussed in this book.

I hope you find them useful.

- Frven

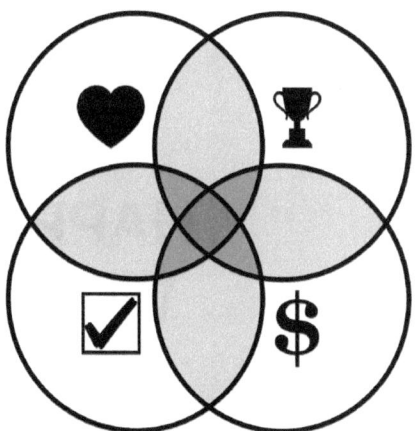

Your notes here

Your notes here

This book is brought to you as part of the objectives of AHA, and is an integral project by the #WHAD movement.

FRVEN.COM
WHAD-FLYT.COM

www.ingramcontent.com/pod-product-compliance
Lightning Source LLC
Chambersburg PA
CBHW060501080526
44584CB00015B/1506